The Basic Essentials of
WOMEN
IN THE OUTDOORS

by Judith Niemi

Illustrations by
Eric Gossler

ICS BOOKS, INC.
Merrillville, Indiana

THE BASIC ESSENTIALS OF WOMEN IN THE OUTDOORS

Printed in U.S.A.

Published by:
ICS BOOKS, Inc.
1370 E. 86th Place
Merrillville, IN 46410

Library of Congress Cataloging-in-Publication Data

Niemi, Judith.
    Women in the outdoors : the basic essentials of / by Judith Niemi.
      p.   cm. -- (Basic essentials series)
    Includes bibliographical references.
    ISBN 0-934802-56-4 :
      1. Outdoor recreation for women. 2. Women naturalists.
    I. Title: Basic essentials of women in the outdoors.
GV183.N54 1990
   796'.0194--dc20
                                       90-31389
                                           CIP

TABLE OF CONTENTS

1. WOMEN IN THE OUTDOORS

"American girls are noted the world over as participants in all kinds of healthful, enjoyable outdoor sports ... By all means, girls, insist on going along ... Let me say, try it once; you'll have less doctor bills, and will thank me on every trip you take thereafter." Francis Buzzacott, The Complete American and Canadian Sportsman's Encyclopedia of Valuable Instruction, 1929.

"The best gift of the Rocky Mountains is nothing less than the transformation of life. Therefore my advice is instant to all inquirers: Go, by all means, go! ... Camp out a little for practice, if possible; if not, go just the same ... You will reach heaven a better person." Zephine Humphrey, "Five Women on the Trail," Outing magazine, 1909.

This book is dedicated to two ideas: that a lot of women would like to feel closer to nature; that the time we spend travelling around and camping in the wilds makes us happier, rowdier, bolder, more uppity. More ourselves. That is true of the hundreds, maybe thousands, of outdoor women I've met, and I'm willing to bet the outdoors would work the same way on millions of others who just haven't tried it yet.

But why an outdoor book for women? Don't women start fires, use a compass and pitch a tent like anyone else? Yes, pretty much. Skills and techniques are mostly the same for men and women — 90%, let's say. This book isn't about that 90%. I'll discuss specific techniques occasionally, when I know women often have questions or concerns about them. But this book is mostly about what's different in equipment, methods, styles and attitudes.

So, about those differences. Well, our bodies are different, obviously, and there are biological advantages and disadvantages for both sexes. But women are at an artificial disadvantage if they are using equipment designed for men's bodies, as it often is. In teaching ways of doing things, instructors don't always take into account differences in size, shape or build. So this is a book of resources, a guide to finding equipment and information meant for women.

And there are cultural differences. It's irrelevant whether we think these are innate or acquired, but all those different social, moral, and psychological characteristics of women show up in outdoor life. Some women decide they don't care for camping just because they've been on trips where they fished a lot more hours than they cared to, or travelled too fast, or didn't get to make many of the decisions. They have not been on co-ed trips, but on men's trips with a few women invited along. It can take a while for a woman to figure out what *she* really likes in the outdoors. This is a book about some ways of doing things and attitudes that work for many women. Camping isn't so much about skills as it is about attitudes, egos, dreams and myths.

For fifteen years I've been guiding women's wilderness trips, and some mixed-gender trips, and teaching outdoor classes. Many of the women have been absolute beginners to outdoor life. From them I've learned a lot about how eager women are to feel comfortable in the outdoors, and about why it can be very difficult for women who haven't had the luck to grow up with wild places nearby and the encouragement to go there. I think of this as sort of a trouble-shooting book, dealing with the most common questions and worries. My own passions are canoeing and living in northern wilderness places; I've also collected ideas from friends and colleagues who have other specialties, and who share this missionary impulse to recruit new women to the mountains, prairies or oceans, to the places and activities we love.

The same concerns come up again and again. "I don't want to hold everyone back." "I'm afraid I can't do my part." "I'm too old, overweight, out of shape, inexperienced, wimpy, other." (Circle one, or more, or supply your own criticisms.) Forget it! You don't have to be taller, stronger or younger to be "the outdoors type." Outdoor life isn't a competition. (Well, you don't have to join the people who collect points and compare records.) It's a most natural thing (although not all that common) for human beings to love the natural world, want to live closer to the other animals, and delight in seeing new places. Maybe you're not in the best condition or training for it. So what? You might as well start now, where you are. The important qualifications are an adventurous spirit and curiosity.

Let's put outdoor skills in some perspective. Most of the people who have walked this planet haven't lived in permanent houses, with porcelain plumbing and mechanical transportation. "Camping out" is often just relearning things our foremothers had to know, things women in other parts of the world do all the time. When some people get enough wealth and leisure, then outdoor life becomes "recreation." It was about a hundred years ago that various outdoor pursuits (often referred to as "manly pursuits") became popular and fashionable in this country; the ladies, of course, weren't supposed to do any of the more strenuous sports or travels. (Ladies, of course, did, when they could get by with it.) There has been another huge burst of interest in outdoor recreation in the last two decades, including women's outdoor programs springing up all over. But 1970's feminism only made it easier for outdoor women to get organized; women have been travelling adventurously all along. Reading about other women (women like you, not Amazons) who have done the things you dream about is a good way to get fired up. (Appendix 1 offers some suggestions.)

If you were brought up to feel nervous about "roughing it," or "survival," try to think broader. Instead of imagining explorers or adventurers, think of the native people who lived in the "wilderness" — men, women, aged people, tiny babies — and not only survived, but often lived very well. Or go back in your own family until you come to a great-grandmother who knew herbs, or did physical work you find hard to imagine. Or just go back in your childhood to a time you loved climbing trees and hadn't yet run into too many rules about what you weren't supposed to do.

This collection of lists, tips and advice, historical glimpses and opinion is intended to provide encouragement and information for women just starting out. It's not about watered-down "Powder-

Figure 1-1
Over the years attire for outdoor lifestyles have changed.

puff Camping." Once you get started, there's no telling where you'll end up going, whether with men, with other women, or solo. I hope this book will also be useful to experienced outdoorswomen. Men too are welcome to read along. We have an awfully good time on women's trips, and are happy to pass along any ideas you can use on men's trips or when camping with the women in your lives.

In a number of workshops or meetings, men who run outdoor programs have asked how they can be more helpful to their women students. My advice boils down to two things: Never *underestimate* what a woman can do, or be condescending, and never underestimate the difficulties that may make it hard for her to start (family obligations, time, money, lack of physical training, years of being told "you can't"). The same advice applies to women. You can probably do anything you want to in the outdoors, and sooner than you imagine. But when you're just starting out, give yourself a break. Take it easy, have fun, surround yourself with encouraging people, and do it your own way. Go for it!

2. COURAGE

"In spite of the opposition of every friend who was on hand to register a complaint (and those at a distance objected by mail) I proceeded with preparations for riding awheel [bicycling] from Chicago to San Francisco ... I started amidst a chorus of prophecies of broken limbs, starvation, death from thirst, abduction by cowboys ..." Margaret Lelong, Outing Magazine, 1898.

It wouldn't be of any use for me to list good reasons not to be afraid, or try to talk you out of it. Fears are too sneaky for that. I'll just pass on how I think about fear, and danger, and the ethics of taking risks.

We'll be standing on the shore of a wilderness lake; several eager but somewhat nervous beginning canoeists are watching the wind rise, and looking off where the lake meets the dark forest. *"Well,"* I'll say, *"the dangerous part of your trip is over now. Driving here. From here on, we're in a pretty secure place."*

Your chances of being seriously hurt on a camping trip are usually far less than when doing a lot of other things in your life: commuting to work, for example, or washing the kitchen ceiling. Yet women especially often assume that camping is vaguely dangerous; or we'll be criticized by others for "taking foolish risks," if the (unspecified) risks are in the wilderness.

This is sad and very ironic. Travelling in wild country, you are taking calculated risks, often small ones, about matters largely in your own control. You can decide whether to climb a particular cliff, whether to ski or walk down a hill; you can judge what's within your skill and experience. The forces of nature are powerful, but they aren't out to get us. In our city lives, on the other hand, we are surrounded by dangers beyond our control or prediction. After a peaceful time in the wilderness, I'm really jumpy on the freeway, with cars hurtling toward me at terrifying speed, driven, for all I can tell, by maniacs. Accustomed to safe, quiet trails, I walk through empty parking ramps wondering if I shouldn't be carrying Mace because there are people out to get me, just because I'm a woman. Still, until a headline reminds us, we often get numb to the random, everyday danger of "civilized" life. How could we bear to really think about it?

Of course there are dangers in the wilderness, like anywhere else. The biggest one is our own ignorance. We need to learn the environment, to learn not only skills, but habits of awareness and taking responsibility. And we need to take the mystery and romance out of words like "risk" and "danger."

Jesse, an ecologist and botanist who has travelled widely in the Arctic for work and pleasure, grew up in New York City. When she started field research, she said she felt confused about danger. *"Half the men I worked with liked to make everything sound danger-ous, to scare me. The other half said, 'Hey, relax, nothing to worry about.' Now I knew there were things to worry about, but I also knew it wasn't nearly as bad as the macho types wanted me to think."* She started enjoying the outdoors when she met people willing to talk honestly about the dangers, without minimizing them and without hype.

Respect your own fears; don't try to cover them up, and don't get pressured into uncomfortable situations. It's easier for women to discuss fears than it is for most men who've been taught to tough it out. Fear has great survival value. A good outdoor teacher won't laugh at you, but will help you sort reasonable fears from unneces-sary ones. Talking about your fear keeps you from being paralyzed by it, taking stupid chances to deny it, or wasting energy on the wrong worries.

At the risk of alarming some readers with the story, I'll give several examples of what I think are women's ways of being open about fear and trying to deal with danger responsibly, in an extreme situation. Climbing in the Himalayas, at the highest altitudes, is so risky that about one climber in ten doesn't come back. In 1978, when the American women's expedition went to Annapurna, was an exceptionally bad year for avalanches. When some of the women were terrified of crossing an avalanche path, leader Arlene Blum encouraged them to take some time off, although they worried about not doing their part; in a couple of days they returned, still scared but freely choosing to be there. Most important, their fear had not become contagious. Individual climbers often re-evaluated their wish to reach the top against the high risks. Irene Miller, who did reach the peak, had almost resigned, not out of fear for herself, but because her daughter, only 13, still needed her. Two women who could have tried for the summit chose not to because they valued other things more. (One was in love; the other was likely to lose a finger and damage her career.) Two others died in a second very risky summit attempt. It was a tragedy for their companions, but they were the two who had decided that the high risk was worth taking. In all the tension and worry of the expedition, individual choices were respected. It seems to me a sane thing not to value risk-taking for itself, but to constantly examine, as the Annapurna women did, its meaning to an individual life.

Most of us can't imagine wanting to put ourselves in such a dangerous place. But the questions we ask are similar: why am I doing this? are the rewards worth it? what would be the consequences if I mess up? A woman learning white water canoeing woke up one morning miserable with nerves, having capsized twice the day before. A little later, she was smiling, all set to get back on the river. She said, *"I asked myself, 'So what's the worst that could happen?' That's the question I ask in all the rest of my life. Well, considering all our safety precautions, the worst seems to be I could get real wet, and I might feel like a klutz. Big deal."*

As you gain experience, and transfer your confidence from guides or other experienced outdoorspeople to your own judgment, you don't become fearless. You learn to foresee problems and avoid them, to worry about everything, and then do what you can about it. Many of the best accident-prevention techniques seem to come very naturally to most women's groups. Take your time, pay attention to your body and mind, and know when you're too tired for good judgment. Let things follow their own natural time. Don't get so caught up with goals that you don't notice the realities of the moment. Don't be afraid to change your plans, to "wimp out" when your common sense tells you to. Trust your hunches. The same intuition that sometimes tells you not to turn down a dark street can protect you in the wilderness.

OK, what about that rapist or mugger on the dark street, or the dark trail? Is it ever really safe for a woman to travel outdoors alone? I suppose not, but safer than in the city where human predators have an easier time finding victims. The farther you go from "civilization," the more likely you've left behind a lot of dangerous people, and are going to find friends. If you travel alone, and many women do, use the same precautions you'd use anywhere else. Scout the territory. If in a public campground, size up the neighbors, and let the nice ones know you're there. If uncomfortable, move on. In a wild area, you may prefer to simply avoid other people, camping inconspicuously.

Maybe the reason it's so easy to think about wilderness and danger in the same breath is just that the outdoors provides us with such clear and straightforward ways for us to meet our fears, and overcome them.

I've met many quietly brave women doing that on outdoor trips. Janet was very afraid of the dark, and always asked someone to accompany her to the latrine at night. It wasn't bears, exactly, just the idea there might be *something* out there. No one laughed at her. On the last night we sat around the campfire, thoughtfully, remembering that back in the city our friends were in a Take Back the Night march. Suddenly Janet walked down the dark path to the latrine alone, for the first time, saying, *"I'm going to take back this night."*

I think of a woman who learned canoeing in her 70's. "The day I decided to come on this trip," she said, "was the day I saw my brother lying in his casket, not having done half the things in life he always wanted to." It took some nerve for her to paddle stern, to split wood. But the bigger risk she took was an emotional one, confiding in new camping friends about things she hadn't told anyone in 60 years.

I remember a day when five of us were cheering and whooping it up at the bottom of a rapids, and suddenly the sixth woman started to cry. *"I feel terrible. You're all having such fun and I am scared shitless."* It took courage for her to say that. Once she had, and we'd all talked about it, her fears began to diminish. In a few days she was so enthusiastic about rapids that the rest of us were busy holding her back. Many months later, she told me how she had come home and made major changes in her life and relationships. *"I figured all that fear I had wasn't just about the water,"* she said. *"And once I got over my excessive fear of rapids, a lot of other fears seemed to disappear with it."*

3. HAVING FUN

"The long miles which separated me from the world did not make me feel far away — just far enough to be nice — and many times I found myself wishing I need never have to go back again." Mina Benson Hubbard, A Woman's Way through Unknown Labrador, 1908

Realistic Expectations

"There we were, in Paradise, hating each other," said an experienced outdoorswoman, just back from her dream trip in the Northwest Territories. The trip had been full of wonderful scenery, new experiences and inner growth, but the conflicts and tensions among the campers were a bitter disappointment. One of the better-kept secrets of outdoor life is how often people have a perfectly miserable time with each other. It's not surprising. You've planned a dream vacation, and find out that others' dreams aren't identical. Just when you want to slow down and appreciate things, someone insists on pushing on. When you want to go for it, someone is a wet blanket. Throw in egos, fears, exhaustion, and even one day of rain, and it gets hard to fix things. But we don't talk about this a lot, because usually the trips are so great in other ways. Anyway, who wants to come home and tell the neighbors that the Big Trip was a bummer?

11

Figure 3-1
In the company of friends paddling is less work and more fun.

No matter whom you go camping with, friends, family, clubs or organizations, your best insurance against disappointment is to take time in advance to see if you have compatible ideas on what a trip should be like, and to see how flexible you all are about your wants.

Family and friends can be the most fun, and/or the most difficult companions. If you haven't camped together before, or are planning a longer or more difficult trip, check out your camping compatibility carefully. You could start with questions like: "What's your idea of 'early'? How many hours a day do you want to be moving on? Why? What's your pet peeve on trips?" Take it from there. I think a whole questionnaire would be a good idea. With some imagination, you can have variety in the days of a trip, but you have to start with being clear on what everyone wants!

If you're going with children, you'll generally have to put their needs first; in distance, scheduling, food. Even with quite grown children, many parents find it most satisfying to take them separately, so each child gets special attention.

An adventure travel company or outdoor program should have its style and goals well defined, so carefully read everything in their brochures, and between the lines, and ask questions. Will they teach you outdoor skills or pamper you? Which do you want? Do they focus on learning about nature? on building your character through challenge? on fun? What kind of people typically come on the trips? Don't wait until the trip to find out that while you wanted to learn navigation, the tour company won't let you in on their route plans, or to find that you're the only middle-aged woman with a group of college boys. Don't be shy about asking for references or information on their guides.

An informal, volunteer outdoor organization may provide teaching, but don't assume that. Often beginners, understandably, expect or hope to be taught, while the "old-timers," also understandably, are out to enjoy themselves with other experienced people. Find out what the leaders intend, and whether the trips are rated in terms of difficulty or speed of travel.

Tips from Women's Trips

The outdoor programs run by women, for women, that have sprung up all around the country in the last fifteen years have a lot of similarities in philosophy and style. This isn't because we all sat down at a conference to decide The Correct Feminist Way, though a lot of us do stay in touch with each other. It just evolved, naturally, from following our own ideas and seeing what works. Maybe because of this pragmatic approach, one of the things that's really common on women's trips is having a terrific time.

All-women trips aren't automatically better than other arrangements, but they do give women a chance to find their own ways to do things. Beginners on easy trips and experienced women on challenging adventures often have similar values; many of these ideas also work just fine on mixed-gender trips. Here, oversimplified, are a few of the values and techniques common in women's programs; take what you can use for your own trip planning.

1. Inclusiveness. Women's programs often try to welcome a variety of women, in experience, background, lifestyle, age, income, class and race. Not all of these are easy to achieve, but many have been successful in attracting "older" women, and this *doesn't* mean over 30, it more often means over 50, or in their 70's. The important part is to have everyone feel welcome as she is, to enjoy the diversity. *"We don't have a generation gap,"* said one young woman on a trip where ages ranged from 25 to 70. *"We just have a whole lot of information we didn't have before."*

Figure 3-2
Share decision making.

2. Non-competitiveness. We can get about as much stress and competition as we want in our everyday lives. On women's trips, there's not much emphasis on "making miles" or proving toughness. Difficult physical tasks don't get more status. "This is the first time I've been on a trip where the canoe carriers weren't the elite," said one woman, with relief. Any little contests that come up (getting the tents up fastest in the rain, impromptu touch football with a sponge) come from spontaneous high spirits, not a plan.

We promote a non-competitive attitude toward nature, especially when doing strenuous or challenging things. Women mountaineers don't talk of "conquering" a mountain (a pretty silly term). When we run rapids (rather than "shoot" them) I like to think of the river as the third partner, the strongest of all of us.

3. Supportive atmosphere. My brother-in-law returned once from a camping trip saying the women had had more fun. "They didn't seem to have expectations for themselves, so they could encourage each other and feel really satisfied when they learned to do something. Some of the guys were into proving they knew things, even if it was all new to them, so they couldn't accept any praise." A hot-dog competitive kayaker was really excited after her first all-women trip. "It was great! I was used to running a rapids and having no one say *anything*. Unless you messed up — then you got razzed. But the women were always cheering each other on, 'Good run!' And when I capsized, they were still cheering, 'Great swim!'"

We get rather carried away with this. On a log-cabin building course, I noticed that all work on the wall had stopped. A small woman was using a maul to slam down some old scaffolding, and five others had gone to be a cheering section. "Go, Deb!"

4. Individual choice. Most women have a healthy streak of anarchy in us. We're highly sensitive to others in a group, but we don't take well to regimentation. In an interesting documentary film of women on a highly structured trip, the group was sent on an un-guided hike for which they felt unprepared. "I feel like I'm being tested," said one woman. "And I don't like it." Deciding to come on a trip or not shouldn't be the last choice you get to make. When challenging activities are offered, it means more if you participate out of free choice. Most women leaders say they try to provide a lot of encouragement and no pressure.

5. Shared decision-making. A group needs leadership. It doesn't need A Leader, as in "Take me to your leader," the guy who runs the show. Most of the daily decisions campers make don't require much expertise — where to stop for lunch, how far to go tomorrow. An experienced leader's job is to see that everyone has the crucial information to facilitate a decision getting made, and see that the plans everyone helped make get carried out.

Most women are comfortable with leadership as a shared responsibility, but questioning authority can be a touchy topic in some outdoor circles. I remember a strange argument I once got into with an outdoor safety instructor who insisted that a group must always have One Leader. But only minutes earlier, he had been telling about the tragic death of a guide to hypothermia — no one had noticed he was becoming disoriented and acting in a peculiar way. If the other people had been accustomed to exercising judgment and responsibility, I thought, the leader probably would not have died; certainly the "leaderless" survivors would have been much safer. *In an emergency* one person takes charge, usually the designated leader or most experienced person. At other times, the more people who are really thinking and deciding, the more leadership there is around.

6.   Creative leadership. Women guides may try to show leadership as a task and function, not a matter of authority. Guides working together may say, "You be the dad today, I'll do the mom stuff, and tomorrow we'll switch." Everyone knows what that means, and the "non-leaders" see the jobs as separate from personalities.

In a "leaderless" group of friends and peers, women's reluctance to step into leadership can be a problem. One woman described it as "like sitting in a circle around the campfire — but there's no fire." Women have found ways to see that leadership gets shared around. One or two may be "on duty for the day," probably not in fixed rotation, but as nominated by others or themselves, as appropriate. One group used a lace-edged bandanna as a daily rotating award to recognize contributions of group members. On one trip everybody was made a boss of some kind. There were the dad roles, like map reader, and time-keeper, but also people in charge of other important matters: a trip naturalist, a sun-worshiper, a reader.

Figure 3-3
Periodically, take time to stop paddling and rest.

7. Playfulness. I'm not going to do anything so cloddy as give suggestions on how to be playful. This is just a reminder that the outdoors is a perfect place to let loose the impulses that got stifled about the time people started telling us to act our age. (How I remember a night that the women over 50 got into singing old show tunes — "Honey, you've never heard of Deanna Durbin??" — and tap dancing on the sand. The teenagers partying nearby had to ask *us* to pipe down.) I've noticed that the most playful groups are often the ones most likely to have intense and intimate conversations. That's the other side of this freedom, an openness to one's most serious and perceptive self.

Which One Is "Real Life?"

What results from all the ways women choose to do our outdoor lives? We find ways to become more ourselves. Camping is not a collection of skills to be mastered, but an open-ended kind of growing. Returning to "the real world" can be painful; especially on long or intense trips, it's a good idea to talk about what going back will be like, and to think about how to keep alive the lessons of the outdoors. What kind of lessons? One of the obvious ones is self-confidence. "If I did that, I can do anything." Maybe it's creating a culture more to our liking than the one we live in. The head of a women's studies program once commented, *"What we do in the classroom is the theory; what women invent together outdoors is the practice — you get to live it out."* For some women, the lesson is feeling like part of nature again. I remember a woman from Brooklyn building her first fire by a northern lake and saying, *"I feel like I'm remembering all this."*

As I was writing this, I happened into a phone conversation with a stranger in California, who described herself as a 5-foot, 100-pound hiker. *"When I'm in the mountains,"* she said, *"is the only time I'm in a place that's BIG enough for me."*

4. HYGIENE: TAKING CARE OF YOUR BODY

"We were told that we looked terrible. We knew that and demanded something to eat. Then there was a lot of business with soap and hot water, to make us feel equal to those large soft beds ... 'Doesn't that feel good? After sleeping on the ground for so long!' We did not wish to be impolite, but we were hot and restless the whole night, feeling stuffy." Anna Kalland, *"It Can't be Done," Outing* Magazine, 1923.

Washing Up

Don't be deterred from camping by thinking you'll always feel unkempt and unwashed. There are quite a few women who, under any camping conditions, manage to look crisp and neat, very uptown. Some people, I suspect, have a gene for repelling dirt. Here are some miscellaneous ideas on how they do it.

If you just have to have a shower every day, and aren't comfortable away from modern plumbing, stick to day trips, or find parks that have all the amenities, at least until you get used to wilder conditions.

Around water, you could decide on the ritual of a swim or quick dip every day; no matter how cold the water, you'll be glad, later. (My personal record is 33 degrees, for seven seconds. I guess it was worth it.)

Your "one allowable luxury" could be a really nice towel. Others use just a bandanna. Better yet, buy a "sport-sponge" (a new L.L. Bean device) to avoid carrying a damp towel around.

When necessary, you really can do a sponge bath with about a half cup of water, as polar travelers do.

Carry pre-moistened travel towels when around salt water, or in cold conditions.

When you can't wash your clothes, air them whenever possible in sun and wind.

Instead of bar soap, use a concentrated liquid soap. Dr. Bronner's soap, besides providing fascinating reading on its labels, is highly concentrated and is good for many uses, including shampoo; scents like peppermint and eucalyptus do not attract insects. A small piece of pumice soap gets deep dirt off your hands.

Whatever methods of washing you use, NO SOAP, (no, not even biodegradable) goes into the water. Pour out all soapy water well back from any lakes or streams.

Make a big production out of cleaning up sometimes. It can be worth it in morale to take a break from everything else, and make washing a celebration. One way is to rig a tarp or plastic sheet over a tent frame to make a steam bath. Heat rocks (not rocks that have been in the water) in a fire *outside* the tent, and carry them into the shelter in a cookpot or with forked sticks. Sprinkle water on them very sparingly.

Hair washing is a great morale booster. Camped once in a drizzly Alaskan bog, we spent half a day at it. We heated water on the stove. We rinsed each other's hair, trying to pose like women on Greek urns. Then someone set up a hair-cutting salon, with hilarious beauty-parlor gossip. (In case you ever need to know, it's possible to give a reasonable hair cut with the scissors on a Swiss army knife.) The rainy rest day was pure play, and the next day we were full of energy. A girl can go a long way on clean hair.

As a trip comes to an end, don't let things run down as you think of getting home and washing in real hot water. Try to keep yourself and your gear in as good shape as at the beginning, prepared to go on for several more days. (This sounds a lot like something I'd have learned in Brownie Scouts. I'm not sure why it feels like such a good idea. I think it's about really making the outdoors your home.)

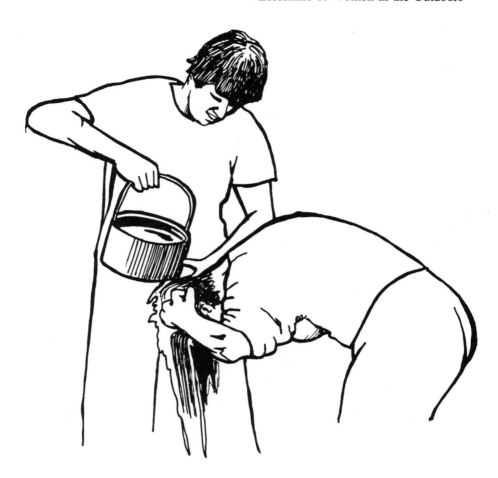

Figure 4-1
Washing hair is much easier with help.

OK, I'll be honest. Sooner or later there will come times when your hands are covered with permadirt, your hair is a frightwig, and your only clean clothes are out in the rain. When you have no time, energy or resources for getting clean, be philosophical. At least it's honest dirt, not smog and toxic wastes. Have an ugly hat-hair contest. Take comfort — you won't keep getting infinitely grubbier. New dirt wears off old, or, as a scientist with long months of field work explained, "You come to equilibrium with your own dirt."

The Beauty Aids Kit

Some women bring not much more than a toothbrush; others choose some real luxuries. Bring what you need to feel good, including the following:

Unscented soaps and shampoo in buggy country, or insect-repelling scents like citronella, pine tar or rosemary.

Skin moisturizers, any time of year. A good sun screen is important; so is aloe vera or some other after-sun, after-wind creams.

Hand cream — the heavy-duty, industrial strength kind. Lotions containing alcohol will dry out your hands more. Pure lanolin, greasy as it is, works better. Very cold weather demands drastic measures to keep fingers from developing painful cracks. An Arctic airplane mechanic told me he soaks his hands in #30 motor oil! Many of us prefer "Warm Skin" lotion, or bag balm, the stuff you buy at a farm supplies store (a few drugstores have it), in cans with pictures of clover and cows' udders. Guaranteed. Carrying a little jar of cold sore ointment in your pocket also works well, because you'll remember to use it often.

Lip ointments, especially those including a sun screen. On the water in hot weather, or on bright snow, it's easy to get a painful sunburn on your lower lip. I've let it happen an embarrassing number of times. My friend Pam, looking at my Victorian lady "bee-stung" pout, had the solution. "I carry five chapsticks. In my pants pocket, my jacket pocket, my day pack, my tent pocket, and a little pocket I sewed onto my sleeping bag for kleenex."

Your Period

Your period is probably going to come early, especially if you go on a long trip with other women. Always carry supplies. Small tampons are the handiest, but if you bring some pads too, they make good emergency compresses to augment your first aid kit. What do you do with the used tampons and pads? Burn them, if possible, (this will take a really hot fire,) or carry them out. (Pack along little plastic bags; put a used tea bag or crushed aspirin in with them, they say, to reduce the odor.) DON'T BURY THEM. Just as household dogs love to raid bathroom wastebaskets, woodland animals will be curious and dig them up.

What about the Big Question? Worried women ask me often:
Is it dangerous for a woman with her period to be in bear country?
No more than for anyone else. Most people's fears are unnecessary,
since 99 + % of the bears campers meet are black bears (even though
they may be brown in color). Black bears aren't in the habit of
attacking people. Attacks have occurred, but so infrequently that
an *unprovoked* and *serious* black bear attack is abnormal. Psychotic
bears are a lot less common than sociopathic humans. What interests
black bears is your food, not you, so avoid bear hassles by keeping
a clean camp, and hanging or hiding your food packs.

Brown bears, or grizzlies (now found only in a few parts of
the Rockies, and in western Canada and Alaska), are another story.
They are by nature aggressive, and can be dangerous to our species.
(Polar bears may be even more so, but camping out in polar bear
country is way past Basic Essentials!) They are most dangerous
when familiar with humans, and crowded, as in Yellowstone. If
you camp in bear country, you owe it to yourself to learn all you
can about their habits, how to avoid them, and what to do if attacked.
But if you're a woman between adolescence and menopause, don't
get into special bear paranoia. There is no evidence that menstruation
has anything at all to do with the serious, but infrequent, brown
bear attacks. Actually, many human odors are known to attract
bears — sexual odors, perfumes, toothpaste, interesting human
food. In other words *everyone* who enters bear territory should be
respectful of their power, stay out of their way and learn good bear
manners.

Other Body Processes

Drink enough water — it's crucial to staying healthy outdoors
(or in the city). Coffee and tea don't count, just water. Being
dehydrated makes you cranky and irritable, and contributes to
headaches, bad judgment, hypothermia and constipation. If you
don't urinate for hours, or if your urine is intensely colored (pay
attention to this), you need to drink more.

You can't rely on uncontaminated water sources, so you need
to either carry water, use a filter, or boil water. Especially when
it's cold, you can forget to drink, so make plans to get enough
water. Fill your water bottle and be sure it's all gone on schedule.

Now, when you do drink enough, the natural consequences are a little more inconvenient for women than for men, especially in the snow, or among mosquitoes, or when there's not much privacy. This is really a very minor problem, although it's amusing that it has been raised as an obstacle to having women on expeditions: "But what about excretory situations?" men ask. The solution is obvious: other people can turn their backs. You can improvise a "widdling tin" for the tent. You cannot make a big issue of it. After all, most of the world's women have not had private flush toilets.

Ingenious manufacturers, however, have worried about this matter enough to invent little funnel devices so women too can urinate standing up. I'll confess I haven't tried them, and actually, I don't know anyone who has. A health survey taken among women in cold-weather strenuous sports reported almost no use of them. If you want to try them, a lighthearted "equipment review" in *Women Outdoors* magazine said they were of some limited use, but pointed out that some leak because of poor fit, and "disposable" ones create another potential litter problem.

While we're on indelicate subjects — take care of any digestive irregularities by the way you eat before considering drastic first-aid measures. Change of activity, water and diet often cause mild constipation or looseness: treat one by drinking more and eating more bulky food, or prunes or fresh berries and greens; treat the other by cutting down on food, avoiding solid food, if necessary, then starting on crackers. A common reason for the runs is not infection but over-zealous soaping of the dishwater with inadequate rinsing. *Giardia* (a main reason for filtering water) can be a serious disturbance, but it usually won't hit you until you're back home.

The trivial camping question that seems to bother most people is — how much toilet paper shall I bring? One correct answer is none, since natural substitutes are available. Here's another correct answer, one many people prefer: bring enough to make people comfortable, but use as little as possible, and leave none behind. Tuck part of a roll and several little plastic bags in your day pack. Burn toilet paper at the cat-hole where you use it only if that is absolutely safe, or burn it in the fire, or pack it out. DO NOT bury it. The natural organic matter you leave behind will, if disposed of properly ("properly" varies with the terrain), decompose from the action of soil microbes or sun. Toilet paper lasts too long, a disgusting reminder of the weirdness of people too squeamish not to use paper, but not a bit squeamish about leaving it ornamenting the landscape.

Avoiding Injury

Women have several assets here. We generally pay attention to our bodies; we're willing to ask for help; we aren't likely to try to prove ourselves through showing off our feats of strength. Aside from learning to do physical motions correctly, and practicing common sense, the best accident prevention is knowing your limits and stopping in time. The end of the day is when tiredness or hurry or the Home Free Phenomenon can make you careless.

Avoid many minor sprains and strains and sore muscles by stretching. When you get up, before lifting or hard walking, do slow easy stretches to loosen your muscles. At the end of a day of exercise, stretch again to get kinks out. Exchange back rubs, or neck rubs.

Getting in Shape

Don't wait until some mythical time of better fitness to start whatever outdoor fun appeals to you. The body you have now, whatever shape it's in, is the one ready for use. Women have a habit of apologizing for themselves, but those who've called themselves, "marshmallowy, but resilient," or who have said, "My enthusiasm for this trip is exceeded only by my flab," have had a wonderful time, even on strenuous camping trips. It's true, of course, that you'll enjoy physical activities more if you're really conditioned for them, but the best training is usually doing them. Once you're having fun, the motivation to get in shape will probably follow.

Resources

Everyone, women or men, should have basic knowledge of first aid for camping, or for city life where accidents are more likely. Red Cross training is widely available. These courses are based on the assumption that medical aid is easily accessible, so try also to to take some classes specifically designed for wilderness first aid. Two good reference books of extensive medical information for a lay audience are: *Medicine for Mountaineering*, edited by James A. Wilkerson, 3rd edition, 1985, The Mountaineers., and *Wilderness Medicine* by William W. Forgey (1979, ICS Books), which is especially useful in setting up first aid kits.

An excellent resource on fitness is *The Outdoor Woman's Guide to Sports, Fitness and Nutrition* by Jackie Johnson Maugham and Kathryn Collins, M.D. (1983, Stackpole). There are sections on hiking, water travel and skiing, exercises for specific activities, and much information on women's physiology. (It is, unfortunately, out of print, but may be available in your library.)

For further hygiene information, see *How to Shit in the Woods* by Kathleen Meyer (1989, Ten Speed Press, Berkeley), which has a special chapter for women. If you're inhibited about doing it outdoors, read this. It's rowdy, explicit, very funny, and her advice is environmentally sound.

5. CAMPSITES

Until you have the experience to feel really at home in the outdoors, it's helpful to provide yourself with enough physical comfort that you also can feel emotionally comfortable and relaxed. Doing that is pretty easy.

Housekeeping

It's a well-kept secret: about 90% of "camping skill" is really just housekeeping, the unimpressive little routines that most women handle like old pros. Picking up after yourself; knowing where to find things; seeing work to be done; being able to juggle five jobs at once. We don't even think of calling all this "skill." The most urban woman is halfway to being a good camper if she has that habit of attention to detail. Even if you hate housekeeping, outdoors it's simpler and more fun.

"A place for everything." Apply Mom's rule to packing: Be compulsive. Exactly where things go doesn't matter much, as long as every day, every trip, your flashlight is in the same pocket, the first aid kit in the same stuff sack, so you can find things as automatically as in your own cupboards.

Carry a purse — a small day pack, or a fanny pack — with all the things you need to have readily with you (raincoat, matches, sunscreen, compass). If you leave it packed all the time you'll be ready to go off on day trips on a moment's notice; tuck it in the top of a larger pack when you go overnight.

Organize the campsite, too. Instead of dropping things anywhere, size up the site. Then be bossy if necessary (it will be necessary if you have kids along): "No personal gear in the kitchen! Just food and pots. And don't tromp on those flowers. Keep the dining room clear." Expect some comfort and elegance in a campsite.

Making yourself at home anywhere. Good campsites are easy to find if you define one as 1) any place that you can take some time to enjoy, or 2) any site that's available when you're about ready to drop. In many well-travelled areas you'll be required to stay at designated sites, so your main job isn't picking a place, but stopping before you find "no vacancy" signs everywhere. As you travel farther from the beaten path, where there are no established sites, it helps to have imagination. It's a real talent to say with enthusiasm, as my friend Connie once did, "Oh, good! We can camp right here in the aspen glade!" when any fool could see we were on a mudflat — a sphagnum bog camp some people thought of as "a swamp," but Kathy called it "Merlin's Enchanted Forest." Well, any old port looks good sometimes, but to live in the greatest number of really spectacular campsites, be flexible. Don't pass up a beautiful place just because you had planned to head for some other dot on the map, or "cover miles."

Camping handbooks of previous generations devoted many chapters to "pioneering" activities: lashing tables, digging trenches around tents and building elaborate balsam bough beds; all unnecessary, and now generally recognized as inappropriate and harmful. I suspect the real reason for all this nesting activity was insecurity, changing the face of nature to be able to lay some kind of claim to a place. Another way to fulfill this nesting impulse and make a connection with a place is by quiet time. If you lean against a tree dreaming, or fall asleep in the sun, this place stays in your mind a long time.

Setting up camp — getting your priorities right. To many people, it seems only logical and correct to get all camp chores done first, then relax. Work ethic. The "work," as always, can be counted on to fill all available time. Ignore that rule when you can get by with it. Decide what you want to do first. Most people (especially teenagers and beginning campers) have a strong urge to get their beds ready, first of all. There's no point trying to get their attention on group tasks like cooking or hanging tarps until their tents are up and belongings are stashed. On the other hand, some experienced campers and free spirits, when arriving at a campsite, want first of all to wander around and explore. We *might* be willing to do minor useful tasks along the way, like picking up a few sticks, but the real point is to get quiet time alone. Talk it over, and whatever is most important to you — swimming, writing in journals, exploring — go ahead, do that while the sun shines. Camping isn't just an exercise in household efficiency, but a time to get out of every day life. Women especially need to remember to stop doing the housekeeping and taking care of other people.

Sometimes, however, when rain clouds are coming and dark is gathering, things need to happen fast. That's a time for someone to take on the job of benevolent dictator, seeing that during the scramble to set up beds, other important jobs don't get neglected. For example, a higher priority might be to put a tarp over all the gear; or to get a stove lit and start cooking — at least soup — right away, before everyone is too tired to bother. Or someone might need to play Mom and order chilled and tired people into dry clothes right away. These very obvious things are easy to forget. I seem to remember that more than once I've been hunched under the dripping trees unhappily grumbling at a balky stove until someone reminded me loudly that I had forgotten to change clothes. Of course — one of the distant early warning signs of hypothermia is stupidity.

Dividing up camp tasks. Back at Girl Scout camp, we had complicated "caper charts" to divide all jobs fairly, but I hardly know any adult women who get formal about assigning tasks, or who like it when someone does. When women camp together, everyone usually just pitches in, doing what they enjoy or want to learn, or the grubby job they haven't helped with lately. Women are so responsible that getting things done is no problem; it's more likely that everyone works unnecessarily much. In an informal way, pay attention to how things get done, if only to be sure that people get time away from housekeeping without feeling guilty. "It doesn't take all six of us to cook. We need two volunteers to keep an eye on the sunset."

Fire

Do you even need or want a fire? Cooking is often easier on a stove. Wonderful as it is to stare into a campfire, evoking ancient memories of the dawn of our species, it's also nice to be friendly with the dark. Watch the stars, listen to the night sounds. When fires are appropriate and can be used without danger and without damaging the environment, build them no bigger than necessary.

Afraid you'll lose face because you can't make a "one-match fire?" All fires start with one match, plus good tinder and patience. (It's just that sometimes a lot of other matches are wasted on premature starts.) Bring plenty of matches, squirreled away in several separate waterproof containers. Give the fire patient attention, nurturing it as you would a relationship.

Start easy, build it gradually. Coddle it along from a tiny spark of interest, to a nice little flame, to a fire big enough to warm you. It's a process, not a one-shot task. Don't pile everything on in the first few minutes.

The logs need to be close enough to share body heat. (You might also need to insulate your fire from snowy or wet ground.) But they also need space to breathe. Don't let them smother each other.

Keep introducing new interests, new larger wood. Without growth, the fire will die.

Fire building is a high-status skill, a popular camp chore. If you camp with others who are much better than you at fire building, con them into being your teachers. If you are a good fire builder, don't monopolize the job; get your fun from teaching others. Once you're good at one-match fires, try using a flint and steel instead (modern versions are available at camp stores), just because it's fun.

Forbidden Skills

Here's a list of several skills that many women shy away from, the ones they haven't been encouraged to learn. If any of these jobs don't seem like women's work to you because the women in your family didn't do them, or if they are mysteries to you, start learning them, one at a time, from books or other people. They aren't particularly hard, and are mostly fun to do. They can be important to camp comfort, and they are the skills that really build confidence.

Splitting wood. (Not chopping trees — just splitting logs so you can start fires in any rain.) For safety, get a good instructor to coach you. Start with easy wood (soft wood, short pieces). I think of it as a zen exercise in concentration; other women say cheerfully that using an ax is really therapeutic.

Sharpening your knife or ax. Just get a whetstone, oil, and a file if you are using an ax, and start practicing. Dull tools make you feel inept.

Starting and tinkering with the camp stove. 95% of what gets a stove working right is pumping and more pumping. The rest is oiling gaskets, and learning a few simple parts.

Knots. When you aren't sure of your knot, don't add more on top. The goal is one good knot that you'll guarantee (test it) and that comes out easily — not macrame. I can't remember any knot that doesn't have an animal ditty, for example, The Rabbit (bowline) and The Gopher (power cinch). I'll include them, since these two can take care of most of your needs and using only two as a start means you'll remember them.

The bowline:

Make a rabbit hole (like writing a 6) ...

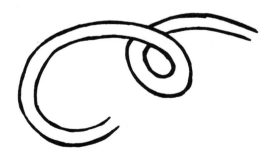

the rabbit comes up out of her hole ...

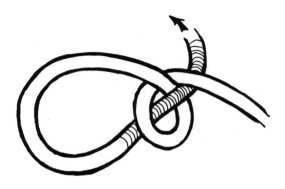

runs around the tree ...
and zips back down into the hole again (now pull tight).
(This makes a loop — any size — that will not jam or get smaller.)

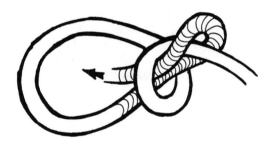

The power cinch, or modified trucker's hitch (I think of it as
Janet's Knot, from the canoe outfitter who first showed it to me):
Make a gopher hole (same as rabbit hole) ...

and a gopher underground (loop of rope) ...

the gopher pops up out of her hole ...
and the end of rope goes through the gopher's head, and is tied off.
(Use this to tie tarp or tent ropes, to fasten gear onto car tops.)

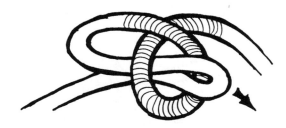

Map anxiety. One last, surprisingly common "forbidden skill:" I've heard many women say, "Oh, he plans the route, and I plan the menus." But knowing maps is the nicest way to dream and scheme new trips. It gives you a lot of control over the kind of trip you'll have ("Hey, isn't that a shortcut? There is too another campsite close to here.") Finding your way can be fascinating puzzle-solving, not to mention how much safer it is if everyone is following the map!

Sleeping Well

Years ago, I used an army-surplus down bag, "mummy" style, laid right on the rocks, and thought only softies used air mattresses or these new self-inflating foam pads. About the time my back was my back was forty years old, I saw the light. Here's what will get you a good night's sleep:

A *waterproof ground cloth.* If you are using a tent, use an extra plastic sheet *inside* the tent, not under it.

A *sleeping pad.* Self-inflating open cell foam enclosed in a nylon waterproof case ("Thermarest" or other brands). Unless you're very tall, you don't need the long one. Just put extra packs or clothes under your feet. Closed cell foam (blue foam, ensolite, black foams) are also warm, but offer less padding.

A *decent sleeping bag.* Not a "4-season" bag, which is too warm for summer, but one suited to the seasons when you usually camp. Short women find a lot of excess space at their feet — that's extra air for your body to try to warm. Few manufacturers make special short-length bags, but you can stuff extra clothes at your feet to fill that space.

A *flat surface.* This is the most elusive ingredient in camp beds. If your feet are slightly downhill, you might find it useful to prop something under them, just to trick your body so you don't spend the whole night bracing against sliding.

Dry bed wear, and socks, NOT what you've been wearing during the day.

A *liner,* maybe. In hot weather, a light cotton sheet; in cool weather, a flannel sheet, or bunting liner.

If you and a regular bed partner are also camping partners, definitely get bags with compatible zippers — it is much warmer and nicer. A good combination is one down bag for on top (light and fluffy) and a synthetic bag for underneath (compresses less).

Camp Furniture

When you are "getting away from it all," don't take it all along. Experiment with how little you really need or want. On the other hand, don't assume that you are supposed to be uncomfortable.

The tarp. Tarps are almost essential to comfort in rain or hot sun — a tent may be optional. Get a good-sized one, light weight coated nylon; if it doesn't already have a lot of grommets and tie-points, add some so you can pitch it a variety of ways.

The sit-upon. Remember that old Girl Scout standby, the Sit-Upon? At least two troop meetings could be devoted to cutting

Figure 5-1
A tarp is essential for protection against the elements.

squares of oil cloth, folding newspapers and stitching it together
with the blanket stitch. Nowadays you can keep it simple by buying
closed-cell foam for insulation from the cold damp ground.

Chairs. Now we're talking real luxury. Heresy, too. Purists
will scorn them, but when it's possible for you to bring a short-legged beach chair or canvas chair, you could probably rent it out by
the minute. Friends who canoed down the entire Yukon were a
little embarrassed about their beach chairs until they met an Alaskan
woman, paddling the river alone, with *her* lawn chair. Older people
especially appreciate the comfort.

Actually, I don't carry chairs along myself, I'm just advocating
open-mindedness. Out on Lake Nipigon, I was amazed to find that
a highly experienced sea kayaker brought along a small umbrella.
"An *UMbrella?*" *said the rest of us. "C'mon, an umBRELLA?*
You're kidding!" She wasn't. Said it's great for reading maps or
taking a squat in the rain.

Now Leave Home

Once your cozy camp is arranged, get out of it. After all, if your main goal was comfort, you could have stayed home and looked at nature programs on TV. Don't get so obsessed with camp skills and chores that you forget why you came. Wander around looking for animal tracks, bedding places and scat; notice what plants grow in your area; fish, hike up the nearest hill, or go for a midnight walk. You'll find a lot of campsites where the earth is packed flat, and the spirits or litter of previous campers are everywhere. Pack up their litter in your extra garbage bag, and then, unless you're in fragile alpine meadows or other areas where you shouldn't leave the trail, ramble around. Most campers seem not to go 50 yards from their tents, so you'll find your own, unmarked places. Expand into all that space around you.

Resources

Among the vast number of good books on camping skills, the most useful will be those specific to your ways of travel and your geographic area. An excellent reference books on low-impact camping in many different environments are *Soft Paths* by Bruce Hampton and David Cole (1988, Stackpole Books). June Fleming's *Staying Found: The Complete Map and Compass Handbook* (1982, Vintage Books, NY) and Cliff Jacobson's *The Basic Essentials of Map and Compass* (1988, ICS Books, Inc., Merrillville, IN) are practical, down-to-earth cures for map-anxiety.

6. CLOTHING

"No woman knows, until she tries it, what a relief it is to travel in the woods without a skirt and without big baggy bloomers to catch on everything." Rena Phillips, "A Woman on the Trail," Outing Magazine, 1904.

Corsets to Goretex: The Evolution of Camping Clothes

In our great-grandmothers' day, a woman — that is, a *lady* — who liked outdoor adventure had a real problem with clothes. (Indian women and rural women who routinely lived and worked outdoors were a bit less oppressed by fashion.) Trousers were too "dreadful" to consider, and ladylike garments weren't made for action. In 1901, mountaineer Annie Peck warned women it was dangerous to wear corsets for climbing; the same year a free-spirited canoeist advised women to "leave behind the trammels of conventionality," but the only trammels she meant were whalebone stays and patent leather slippers. Gradually, however, the bolder women, once they got out of sight of towns, started taking off their skirts, under which they were sneakily wearing boys' knickers. Next came the scandalous bloomers, introduced by bicyclists who didn't want yards of material catching in their spokes. Then riding jodhpurs were adopted by fisherwomen. Freedom of movement was being won, slowly. Still, even encumbered by the rather silly looking outfits we see in old photos, these women made some very impressive journeys.

Come to think of it, women wore some pretty silly camping clothes back in the '50's and '60's, when I started camping: perky little sailor hats, with no brim to keep off sun or rain; blue jeans, of course, which stayed wet for days; hooded sweatshirts, which acted like sponges. We were wet and cold a lot, but we had great fun, and many of us got hooked on camping for life.

Next came the army surplus game. Aside from the difficulty of finding women's sizes, surplus stores provided a lot of practical clothes: tightly-woven wool gabardine pants; norwegian army pants with an extra layer on the seat and knees; "jungle pants" with cargo pockets big enough to lose your binoculars and bird book in, ankle strings to keep out insects, and a lot of other little tabs and cords that I have never figured out. Most surplus store outfits were pretty funky. But look, we were serious *campers*, and scorned fashion.

Then, suddenly, only a few years ago, camping was "in." Everybody started manufacturing women's outdoor clothes, first in wonderful earth tones, then in berry colors, then in lemon, purple and hot pink. These days you can pick your outdoor image: Ms. Rambo in army surplus; out of Africa in tastefully rumpled khaki; or fashion queen, every petroleum-based garment color-coordinated.

The lesson of all this is don't obsess about proper outdoor clothing. Wear what makes you comfortable and happy.

They LOOK Like Good Camping Clothes. Are They?

Watch out for impostors, clothes made for The Outdoor Look, not the outdoor life. The Look is all some people want. In an outdoor store I overheard a frustrated sales clerk trying hard to explain the very expensive virtues of a top quality rainsuit to a confused young couple. "But you see," he pleaded, "if you were buying this for *function* ..."

Inferior clothes now have exactly the same problems we used to complain about back when no one bothered to make outdoor clothing for women: They don't put enough pockets in women's pants (can't spoil the fanny-line!); women's clothing sometimes isn't stitched strongly; clothes that look good are cut too tight for real action; shirts and jackets are cut too tight for many women's hips. Look for these details.

A Brief Consumer Guide to Materials and Layers

There are two rules for good camping clothes: buy the right materials for your use; always combine several layers for good protection.

Cotton — a mixed blessing. It grows in Dixie, so use it in hot weather. It breathes well and it cools you down. Soak your cotton hat or bandanna, so the evaporation can cool your body and temper. Wear cotton T-shirts in the summer. Wear a long-sleeved, light weight cotton shirts to keep off sunburn and mosquitoes.

Cotton can also be woven into tough, long-wearing and wind-proof fabrics. It was once much used for tents, and still is excellent in wind-breakers, often combined with synthetics.

Do NOT wear cotton in wet and cold weather. Winter campers put it very concisely: COTTON KILLS! It gets damp easily, stays damp, and cools you right down. (Wet denim sacks made from your cut-off jeans are good "refrigerators" for butter and cheese in

Figure 6-1
Use a handkerchief to shade your face or protect your ears from bugs.

hot weather.) Some winter underwear is cotton, or cotton blends. Don't buy it, or wear it only *after* skiing, for sipping brandy by the fireplace. Don't wear cotton socks when your feet will be in and out of water all day. (Fish-belly feet!) Above all, DON'T WEAR BLUE JEANS FOR CAMPING. Sure, you see denim on campers everywhere, on the Marlboro man, and on Inuit boys by icy Alaskan rivers. That's only because Levi's are promoted and exported as widely as Coca-Cola; it doesn't mean it's good for you. Denim is terrible stuff to be wearing in wet and cold — you'd be warmer nude.

I don't mean to be prejudiced. Some of my best clothes are cotton. It makes lovely soft things like shirts of snuggly flannel or smooth brushed cotton ("chamois-cloth"), which are great for cool dry days or for lounging inside a cabin. But I regretfully leave them all at home when packing for a long canoeing or backpacking trip. A few garments have to cover me in all weathers; flannel and chamois cloth, turned soggy, don't make it.

Wool retains warmth even when wet. For many outdoor clothes you need wool, or a substitute with this property. Loosely woven, wool contains many dead air spaces for insulation; tightly woven, it has great wind resistance. Wool used to be essential for campers' long underwear. (If you are lucky enough ever to find angora [rabbit wool] long johns, snap them up! They have disappeared from the earth.) Wool was crucial for jackets, shirts, hats, gloves, and socks. Now you can choose between wool and synthetics.

Synthetics for warmth and wicking. Once upon a time there was just "pile" — a bulky petroleum product that substituted for wool, dried fast, and wore well. Then the technology improved and new, softer, thinner, nicer-looking fabrics arrived: bunting, "synchilla," "capilene," "thermax," "thermolactyl" and many other proprietary names. There are light, soft synthetics for underwear and heavier weaves for jackets and insulation. They retain warmth when wet, and wick moisture away from your skin at least as well as wool. They dry faster. Especially useful: lightweight liner socks to wear inside wool socks, and long underwear for skiing and other perspiration-producing activities.

Wool Versus Synthetics: A Matter of Personal Preference.
Feel: wool might make you itch; some synthetics feel as cozy as plastic.

Care: wool shrinks; some synthetics shrink to doll (size) clothes in the dryer, or melt over the campfire.

Smell: wet wool doesn't smell great; some synthetics when combined with particular people's perspiration smell like a toxic waste dump. Experiment!

Aesthetics, tradition, sentiment ... I love wool, but notice those fancy new products sneaking into my closet, too.

Fur and feathers. Birds and beasts are dressed just right for their climates. Humans don't have very good pelts, so we steal, killing the original owners. Most anti-fur protests focus on the questionable ethics of fur farming and killing for luxury and status. People who live in severe climates use furs for better reasons: wolverine parka ruffs prevent frostbite; beaver mittens keep a sled dog driver's hands from freezing. Humans could not have survived in polar regions without the furs and meat of animals. Animal lives are also lost for some of the other best products we have: goose down (there's nothing like it for lightweight comfort at 40 below zero); leather (an organic water-resistant and breathable material); sheepskins (good for boot liners and mittens). Synthetics use up nonrenewable petroleum resources. Face it, there aren't many pure, low-impact clothes.

Goretex and other rainwear materials. Nylon — in various weaves — is very tough, is used in windproof garments, and is coated for rainwear. The problem is that in waterproof fabrics you could perspire so much you get wetter from inside than from the rain. Goretex (and other companies' later proprietary fabrics) was invented to be tough and waterproof *and to breathe*, making excellent rainwear for active sports. It is wonderful as a windbreaker; it gets mixed reviews on its waterproof qualities in extreme (or dirty) conditions.

Your rain gear could be your most important purchase. There

are several choices. Use Goretex or other breathables when sweating really matters (backpacking, for instance); expensive. Coated nylon for many uses; much less expensive. "Air-weave" outfits made for construction workers and firemen; cheapest, still very good. For extreme wet, when sweating isn't an issue, rubberized sailors' foul-weather gear is best; usually expensive. Whatever type you choose, get a complete suit of rain jacket and pants, and get them roomy. Sometimes a rain poncho is sufficient; they are nice and cool, and can cover your backpack, but it's hard to be both very active and stay dry inside one.

One last note on fancy rain gear and other jackets: if you have long hair, watch out for the ones with velcro fasteners at the neck!

Plastic. Not cheap, plastic rainsuits or ponchos, which won't last the afternoon — plastic bags. A tough leaf bag can be made into a tunic that's not a bad emergency rain coat. In Alaska, two women wore Hefty raincoats for weeks, when their expensive new rainsuits failed. In a sudden cold rain you can wear a plastic bag inside your clothes as a vapor barrier (keeping your warm body moisture from leaving); it's hypothermia prevention. Heavy bags, often recycled from your eaten-up meals, make fine boot liners when your feet get soaked. If your socks are wet, too, wring them

Figure 6-2
Plastic garbage bags make adequate emergency rainwear.

out and wear the bags inside. One rainy October day, a woman wearing bread bags on both feet, with matching daisies around the ankles, claimed, *"Learning about this was worth the whole cost of the trip!"* Get in the habit of bag saving, and always stash a few extras in your pack or pocket.

The layered look. The first layer is a second skin, which helps wick body moisture away from you; next come insulation layers, holding warm air — the outer layer is your shell, which keeps you and your insulation safe from wind and rain. Your garments should all be cut loosely enough to allow for proper layering, and easily removable, to encourage you to add and subtract layers often. (Before you are too warm, or too cold!) Front zippers are often preferable to pullovers for that reason. Wearing a removable dickey or scarf instead of a turtle neck keeps you from overheating. Your hat is your best thermal regulator; when your feet are cold, put a hat on; take it off to avoid sweating up your clothes. A little day pack or fanny pack to stow the extra clothes in is handy.

Footwear

Walking and backpacking: No one, but no one, wears heavy "waffle-stomper" boots anymore, the ones with red laces that people used to trudge to college classes in. For most purposes, good walking shoes or light boots (all-leather or leather and fabric) are easier on you and on the earth.

Around water, and in camp: Sport sandals are a great new invention; Teva and Alp make tough ones with Velcro straps, or "apostle style" with lots of wrap-around thongs. Most all-canvas boots don't hold up well at all, but the French ones sold by L.L. Bean have been reliable.

Around cold water: Neoprene wet-suit booties are good for a few hours at a time. For longer wear, use knee-high rubber boots with a lot of wool socks and a wool felt insole. (Red Ball boots come in women's sizes.)

Very cold weather: Boots are cold when they are too snug to wiggle your feet with two pair of socks in them. Rubber bottoms are cold. For extremes, use boots with built-in insulation (army "Mickey Mouse" or Korean boots, LaCrosse "Iceman" boots). Real luxury is mukluks. You can get lined, coated nylon ones to be worn over running shoes, or soft leather and canvas ones, with felt or wool liners.

Some Finicky Thoughts on Fabric and Color

"Visual pollution." Some other campers will consider loud "artificial" colors an intrusion. This is pretty small potatoes as environmental concerns go; the animals don't care, or even notice, if you wear hot pink. However, for blending in when you want to get close to animals, wear camouflage or soft plaids, not solid colors.

Photography. Bright "National Geographic red" is the cliche contrast spot among blue and green. Subtle earth tones and deep reds harmonize well. Orange, purple, etc. could look hot and exciting, or just jarring. (Incidentally, any plastic will find its way into as many photos as possible.)

Insect attraction. No one agrees on exactly which colors work, but in general, mosquitoes love blue and most deep rich colors. They are bored by white or tan. Some gnats and flies will swarm all over particular shades of orange, bright yellow or red.

Safety. Life jackets are good in red or yellow; orange, scarlet or pink are obviously the colors of choice if you dare be in the woods during hunting seasons. On the other hand, many women who camp alone or in small groups in heavily travelled areas prefer to be very inconspicuous.

Noise. Nylon, Goretex and some other synthetics rustle a lot. If you want to get close to animals, wear soft, natural fabrics.

The Real World — Advice from the Field

I've given you too many rules; here's what people really do. Several outdoorswomen are talking about what they think beginners should know:

"Too many women don't remember to wear a belt — it's really handy." "I wish we could talk everyone out of blue jeans. Just forbid them. Even running shorts would be better — they dry so fast. Running shorts, with polypro long johns and wind pants. That would be terrific." "I really love pink and purple Norwegian rag wool socks. One pair is always kept in my sleeping bag, only for night wear." "I have a special wool sleeping cap, and a soft flannel nightshirt." "I've started carrying lightweight polypro gloves all the time — when it's not cold, they keep mosquitoes off."

Old-time campers have fun with outdoor clothes. Edith wears — against advice — bib-top overalls she calls "hogwashers" and a straw hat. Kristin wears dashing wide-brimmed, black desperado hats with a feather. Marsha has a cap with a stuffed silver fish swimming through it, and loves awful Hawaiian shirts. When she's guiding, she doesn't wear that outfit on the first day ("I guess it wouldn't help my credibility, would it?"), but by day three, the wild clothes come out. If you can't escape the tyranny of fashion on a camping trip, when can you?

7. Purchasing Equipment Intelligently

Get OUTSIDE! Even if you're an absolute beginner with hardly a crumb of gear, go, have fun, make mistakes, develop the skills and common sense that are more important than any piece of equipment. Along the way, you'll find out what gear you *need* and what gear you *want*.

How New Outdoor Gear Gets Developed

Most new products aren't developed by mega-corporations just looking for anything new to foist off. Here's what often happens. Some outdoor expert applies know-how and new materials to solve his or her own real problems. Often it's one inventive genius with an old sewing machine in the spare room. Trial and error and testing result in wonderful products. The inventor becomes an entrepreneur, forms a small company called Whiffenpoof or Orca and a clever product makes outdoor life easier or safer for a lot of us. Then the small company grows, selling fifteen tent models instead of one, or the inventor gets tired of managing, and sells the mid-size business to a huge corporation. The problem is, now they have to sell a lot of stuff, and have to convince a lot of people to want it.

45

Just Say No

There are several reasons you might not need a perfectly nice piece of gear. If you're trying to resist a purchase, ask yourself:

1) *How did the human race get along without this until now?* Think about pioneers, or native Americans, or less-developed countries where local people use fewer things in a year than many Americans bring for two weeks of travel. I agree some modern products are almost indispensable — plastic bags and duct tape. All the rest is frills.

2) *Do I want it now?* If sophisticated, top-of-the-line gear will help your learning, and if you can afford it, fine. Don't get it if it's more than you can use. Will you feel upstaged by your own equipment, unnerved by too many gears on the bike, worried about keeping the expensive tent clean?

3) *Is a simple design better?* Could I repair this in the field?

4) *Can I improvise?* It's fun to invent and scrounge. Twenty years later, I remember with joy the time that hard-core coffee drinkers forgot all the cups; we spent happy hours developing mugs out of birchbark and baggies. Collect useful items: nurses get used sterile saline bottles (water bottles, for storing milk powder, syrup); my pharmacist saves small plastic stock bottles (matches, spices, soap powder). Don't squelch your own creativity.

The Gear Head on a Budget

Maybe you assume a gear head is usually male, a guy with more money than time to use his toys, and a garage full of boats, fishing rigs and skis. Not necessarily. The essence of the true gear head is not *owning*, any more than all art connoisseurs collect Rembrandts. The real point is to be able to *talk* about equipment, endlessly. If you do love outdoor gear, it's inexpensive to play this game. Outdoor magazines are always running reviews of new equipment, where you can find out more than you ever wanted to know about it. When you do buy gear you'll know the vocabulary and what questions to ask. (If technical details bore you, skip the reviews, but do get advice from experienced people.)

Where to Shop

For the best outdoor clothes, go to an outdoor store with a full range of serious outdoor clothing and equipment, not to a department store. You'll find the extra features that make a difference: covered zippers, large pockets, sturdier construction. For tents and packs, too, shop the outdoor store, not discount stores or gas stations. Cheap gear is often no bargain. It won't last, because of narrow seam allowances, flimsy construction, bad zippers or inferior design.

Look for a store that deals in information as well as merchandise. If there's a well-informed sales staff who are themselves enthusiastic outdoors people, go when it's not busy and ask them a lot of questions.

Some of your gear you can get by spending less. Army surplus gear varies widely in quality, but you often get good values in basic packs, clothing and cook kits. Cheap men's work clothes have worked for thousands of outdoor women. Small town general stores and variety stores often have wool shirts, jackets, leather gloves at much lower prices than urban camping stores. An industrial safety supply store furnishes good, cheap rain gear to half the campers I know.

If you're planning a trip in another part of the country, do some of your outfitting there if possible, for a better selection of gear appropriate to the climate and conditions; you may also find maps or small-press books on the area not available elsewhere.

Advice from the Field

Outdoor gear is fun, and packed with emotional value; memories stick to it along with the mud and sunscreen. People's choices are quirky and personal. To get some perspective, and find out what other outdoorswomen think is really important, I've been conducting a highly unscientific survey. Lounging on sunny riverbanks or around campfires, I've been asking:

"What's your absolutely favorite piece of outdoor gear? The thing that has made the biggest difference to you, that you can't imagine going camping without?"

Here are a few recent answers:

Jane and Pam, canoeing and kayaking friends for many years (in unison): *"Our Tom Thumb insulated coffee mugs! Sixty-nine cents!"* Pam: *"I got to really like camping once I realized I didn't have to drink cold coffee."* Jane: *"Pam's is better. She punched a hole in the lid and tied it on so it can't get lost."*

Elizabeth (enthusiastic mid-life convert to adventurous camping: *"My knife, a little Girl Scout knife my father found in the street and gave to me."* Did you carry a pocket knife before you started camping? *"Oh, no. Never. But now I wouldn't go out without it. At professional conferences, I use it to slice peaches at lunch."*

Jane, self-defense teacher: *"My knife — the one I love for aesthetic reasons is this little honey"* (an elegant, modern design sheath knife). *"I'm going to get some soft leather to cover the case, and do some beadwork on it."*

Nancy, a "self-confessed, practicing Gear Head": *"When we switched from canvas to good nylon tents, it was sheer revelation! I adore tents — they are always coming up with innovations. And then there's the whole bunting-synchilla-capilene continuum. But this year my big new find is a towel substitute, my L.L. Bean Sensi sport sponge."*

Judith, canoeist and photographer: *"My waterproof, earthquake-proof ammo can. I lined it with foam, painted it white to reflect heat, and put fluorescent tape on so I can't lose it. It's the only way my camera is ever accessible on the river."*

Carol, computer wizard and owner of a lot of high-tech gear: *"Ziploc bags ... how could anyone camp without them."*

8. TRAVELING AROUND

Instead of just taking up whatever activities your friends or families already do, you might look around a little. Maybe you're basically a bird, happiest high in the mountains, trying to leave earth behind; or you need water to feel calm and whole; or you enjoy most the company of other species (and maybe hate being a beast of burden yourself) and will love horsepacking, or hiking with llamas. The next chapter is a quick survey of some of the most common ways of non-motorized travel, with encouragement and advice from women who teach these skills, and hints on how to find more good information for women.

HIKING AND BACKPACKING

Walking Your Own Way
Walking is so personal that our speech is full of phrases that recognize its importance and individuality: we demonstrate our convictions in marches, joining with others "from all walks of life," and we empathize with others by "walking a mile in their shoes." Becoming a good walker means finding your own natural pace. Height-weight-age charts won't tell you how fast you should walk.

It depends not only on your physical size and condition, but on temperament. To find your own pace, walk. Do it a lot, preferably alone. On perhaps the third or fourth day of a hiking trip, or in a couple weeks of walks around your neighborhood, you'll "hit your stride," and you'll know it. You feel alive, energetic, you could go on all day. Pay attention to that feeling, cultivate it and recognize it, so you'll get used to walking your own pace, not anyone else's.

Walking with Others

Walking your own pace feels wonderful; playing catch-up to someone else's pace can be miserable. It happens a lot when short-legged people and long-legged people hike together. Lynn Thomas (*The Backpacking Woman*) estimates that while a six-foot man with a three-foot stride covers a mile in 1760 steps, a short woman might have to take 3520 steps, or up to 5000 if she's hurrying. Wonder why short-legged people get tired? It's not fun; it's also not very enjoyable for long-legged people to constantly try to shorten their stride or wait. Something's got to give.

Faster hikers can go their own way, and periodically stop to wait, staying busy with maps, birdwatching, whatever. (Fast walkers must NOT take off as soon as the slower ones come in sight. This causes all kinds of bad feelings. And each person carries his or her own snacks and water! Your feeling of freedom is ruined if your lunch has gone way ahead.) Or, if each person is competent and confident enough, you can enjoy hiking separately all day, only meeting at agreed-upon campsites. Or instead of always planning straight-line or circle routes, you can hike in to a base camp, and from there take day hikes that accommodate different paces and wishes. If you hike with kids, you'll really have to adjust for very short legs — and for children's habits of stopping to investigate everything. Maybe they know something about the reason for walking that many of us have forgotten.

Separate and Equal

In backpacking, or any other outdoor activity, it can be very difficult for a group to divide, by gender or any other way. Of course, you need to be sure it's safe to divide, and have sure ways of finding each other again. I think the reason why many people

Figure 8-1
Daytime trekking attire.

don't is not practical problems, but an unspoken rule: *thou shalt be together always.*

During a workshop for graduate students in experiential education who were travelling around the country together, I asked, "Do the men and women ever divide and do different things?" "Oh, no," they said, slightly shocked at the suggestion. As we talked, it came out that they had divided once, not quite intentionally. A few students, all men, took off fast toward the top of a mountain. Two other groups formed for the day, one mixed group and one all women. As it happened, the men's group hiked fast and took longer rests. The others kept a slower but steady pace, and everyone got to the top at more or less the same time. So there weren't any problems about competition, or egos, or goals; everybody got what they wanted.

"Did you like doing it that way?" I asked, since they were talking about the day with a lot of enthusiasm. The men who'd been together said, *"Oh, yeah. It was a great day. But, well, we did wonder what the women were doing, and felt sort of left out."* The mixed group said the same. The women said, *"Oh, we had a wonderful time. But ... we felt sort of guilty."* They never divided up again. Apparently just the idea of women doing their own things was too threatening.

If you suspect some separate activities (by gender, age, whatever) would make your trips more fun, it's best to start early, before this habit of compulsory togetherness is too strong to break. Don't always divide the same way — enjoy different hiking partners. And don't feel guilty; you aren't rejecting the other people, just choosing more freedom, and often, more peace and quiet.

Backyard Backpacking

Before setting off for famous mountain trails, high altitudes or rough terrain, ease into backpacking. Break in your boots. Test what weight you can carry, and find out how much you can live without. Get in shape by walking to work or on errands. A professor friend of mine used to get in shape for the Sierras by filling his pack with books, and hiking up and down the stairs in his apartment building while grading history exams. Many of us don't have that kind of discipline (and I never did ask if his grading got tougher or more lenient by the 10th floor), but you can make "conditioning" your excuse for great weekend getaways.

I asked backpacking leader Linda Getz what would be her most essential advice to beginning backpackers. Now, Linda's a woman who loves far places so much she took a year off work to celebrate being 50 by hiking in the Sierras, Nepal and Alaska. But her immediate response was, "I'm always telling people, use backpacking to get into wild places close to home. Even in crowded state and national parks, while other people were being turned away, I've gotten in just by saying that I'm backpacking. Often there are good 'backcountry' sites less than a mile from the road.

And no radios or noise." Besides parks, you can visit state forests, or private land, with permission. You'll get to know your own area, and learn the skills and confidence you'll need when you're ready for longer trips.

Equipment and Resources

Good boots or shoes are essential (see chapter 6) but "good" isn't what a sales clerk recommends as top quality, it's what fits *your* feet. For most women, this means buying from a company that builds boots on a woman's last.

Packs, too, are not really gender-free. Don't get one too large. You will normally carry only 20 to 25 pounds of gear (weigh everything!) plus about 1½ pounds per day of food. It's not just total carrying capacity that matters — you want a frame that fits your bone structure. Among the companies that build good packs to women's dimensions are Kelty and Lowe. Coleman makes packs that are adjustable within a wide range, and also produces compact packs designed for small people. Whether you want an internal frame pack (balances better) or an external frame (cooler in hot weather) is up to you. In either, look for a well-padded hip belt to take full advantage of women's wider hips; this really allows the weight to be carried on your pelvic bones, not just on your shoulders and neck.

The Backpacking Woman by Lynn Thomas, (1980, Anchor Books) is full of good how-to information, and also incudes some profiles, history, and thoughts on why backpacking is really valuable to women.

ROCK CLIMBING AND MOUNTAINEERING

Strength Isn't Everything

One image of rock climbing comes from magazine photos — a climber in hot pink and black tights hangs by one straining, sinewy arm over thousands of feet of empty space. "Not for me!" you think. But only a small percentage of climbers are the super athletes, and most climbing is done with many safeguards. You can enjoy climbing and mountaineering at many levels with just general good health and moderate fitness.

"Actually, physical strength is hardly important at all, in any way, for beginning climbers," says Melissa Quigley, a competition climber and climbing instructor. *"It's fun to watch women as they discover that upper-body strength doesn't matter, as they learn the tricks and techniques. It's grace, and finding your center of balance."*

In fact, Melissa believes women may have an advantage in learning climbing. "Some men when beginning just pull themselves up, like climbing a ladder without using their legs. They are so strong, they don't take time to learn the techniques, to learn the dance. Women often have a better sense of their bodies, and they *have* to learn the dance, the balance — it's actually more beautiful to watch."

In climbing and other outdoor skills involving danger, it's important to get good instruction. This can come from friends or informal clubs, but you're likely to make better progress with a qualified teacher. Don't be reluctant to ask for and check references, to inquire about safety records. Should you look for a woman instructor or a women's class? Some instructors believe that they tend not to push their students as hard in an all-women group. Melissa finds the opposite. "When it's an all-women group, women tend to have lots of personal interaction, and be much more supportive. So they *try* harder; there's more chance of working through the fear."

Mountaineering — A Women's Tradition

Women have been enthusiastic mountaineers since the earliest days of the sport, when they climbed in skirts and hobnailed boots, cutting out snow steps with a tin drinking cup. Mountaineering is also about the best-documented of all outdoor adventures. Are climbers more literary, or less private, than other outdoorspeople, or is it just that the drama of many mountain stories makes good reading? Whatever the reason, there is rich literature about women and mountains, and even if you'd never dream of taking up mountain climbing, these books are inspirational reading on the spirit of adventure in women.

Equipment and Resources

In buying or using a safety harness for climbing, be aware that not all of them offer a good fit on a woman's pelvis; get expert advice in fitting it. Technical climbing shoes, like other boots, should be bought not by reputation, but by fit.

Some of the history of women and mountains is in Cicely Williams' *Women on the Rope: The Feminine Share in Mountain Adventure* (London, 1973), a ladylike British view, and in Janet Robertson's *The Magnificent Mountain Women: Adventures in the Colorado Rockies*, (due for publication May 1990, U. of Nebraska Press). A few of my favorite mountain books by women are listed in Appendix I. Arlene Blum compiled an excellent annotated bibliography which is included in her book *Annapurna* (1980, Sierra Club Books). Also Bill Birkett and Bill Peascod have written *Women Climbing: 200 years of Achievement,* 1990, Mountaineers.

BICYCLING

A Sense of History

Bicycling was all the rage about a century ago, but when women enthusiastically joined in, some people were really upset. Conservative gentlemen foresaw (quite correctly) that freedom of movement for women could lead ... well, who knows where? So they raised all kinds of objections: learned men proclaimed bicycling was bad for a lady's heart, delicate female organs and fragile mental health. They were trying to hold back the tide. Today women outnumber men as buyers of bicycles. When you get your bicycle out, think not only of the good it's doing your heart and mental health — recapture the rebellious sense of freedom of those early riders in bloomers, or your own ten-year-old self with your first bike.

"Girls' Bikes"

Since we no longer have to maintain standards of femininity by riding in long skirts, the "women's frame" (or drop frame) is a matter of tradition, not real function. The question is whether you're comfortable swinging your leg over the seat. An elderly gentleman was asked (by some busybody) why he rode a women's bike. He said, with great dignity, *"It's a man's step-through."* Many models of bicycles are not made with drop frames.

Bicycle frames are not, however, "uni-sex" in design. Most of them are proportioned to average men's bodies. Women usually come with shorter torsos, shorter arms, and smaller hands; among the problems bike designs have caused many women is a tired neck, from leaning too far forward over a front tube that is too long for them.

Mechanical engineer Georgene Terry, a builder of custom bicycle frames, found that most of her customers were women, who liked her design features. Besides a shorter top tube, her bikes have smaller handle bars, smaller toe slips and brake levers; on short bikes, good balance also requires a front wheel smaller than the rear one. She began marketing a line of Terry bikes in 1985. Some other manufacturers are also incorporating designs that fit many women's bodies better. Mountain bicycles, which have brought bicycling off the highways and into the back country, are often available in drop-frame design, and some are now available in "compact" models.

Resources and Equipment

Andrew Ritchie's *King of the Road, an Illustrated History of Cycling* (1975, London, and Ten Speed Press, Berkeley) includes a fine chapter on "Women's Liberation" in English bicycling. An excellent how-to book is *The Woman Cyclist: Training and Racing Techniques* by Elaine Mariolle and Michael Schermer (1988, Contemporary Books). Among many stories of women's travel by bicycle, are Barbara Savage's, *Miles From Nowhere*, (1983, The Mountaineers), or Dervla Murphy's *Full Tilt: Ireland to India with a Bicycle*. (See Appendix 2 for other titles.)

For a catalog of Terry bikes and a list of dealers, contact Terry Precision Bicycles, 140 Dispatch Drive, East Rochester, NY 14445.

WINTER SPORTS

Staying Warm

Ability to tolerate cold well is partly genetic. Women have some inherent advantage in having a better layer of body fat for

Figure 8-2
Make sure to dress adequately for winter excursions.

insulation, although this alone won't keep you warm unless you also pay attention to the other factors. These are: getting acclimated (your body takes care of this in time); being in good condition so your body can quickly convert food into heat (training conditions not only muscles, but also your metabolism); knowing a hundred little tricks of dressing and behavior that keep you warm.

Here are a few of these tricks:

1.   *Clothing.* Following fashion usually will ensure that you are cold. Be prepared to look bulky or bizarre; approximately spherical is the right shape for really cold weather. Silly hats and enormous boots can also be crucial. (See chapter 6 for more details on clothing.)

2.   *Eating and drinking.* Even if you ordinarily eat only salads and lean fish, come prepared for winter activity with lots of high-cal snacks; peanut butter, nuts, chocolate, seeds, dried fruit, plum pudding, mince meat. Drink a lot, but not caffeinated coffee or tea, and certainly not alcohol until later, in front of a warm fireplace.

3. *Don't Sweat.* Take off layers, and pace yourself.

4. *Don't ignore a chill.* Put on layers, jump around, eat something right away. At the first sign of frostbite, stop and warm the part. Fortunately, most women are not very inclined to tough it out, ignoring their body's signals. Dealing with cold is not being wimpy — it's a survival skill.

5. *Use insulation when you find it.* When you have to stand around, look for wind shelter. Stand on wood instead of ice. Sit on a foam pad, extra clothing, grasses, anything at hand.

CANOEING

Canoeing, the most popular of "silent sports" on the water, has been called "the very poetry of travel." But while many of us believe canoeing is absolutely fulfilling the purpose of life, there are plenty of women whose experiences on the water have been very unpoetic. Any outdoor sport, including canoeing, does offer a lot of ways to have a rotten time: perceived danger, heavy equipment to manage, lots of opportunities for being yelled at or feeling silly. This is the skill I teach most often, so I'll use it as a case study of how to avoid some of these problems.

A Woman's Place: This Business of Bow and Stern

I've heard hundreds of women say, "Well, I've canoed for several years, but only in the bow." Sometimes, "only in the bow, *of course.*" Or, "I've never been allowed to paddle stern."

This idea that in mixed-doubles canoeing the man is supposed to be in the stern has absolutely nothing to do with good technique, or common sense. It's about status and power. Someplace along the line people got the notion that a 17-foot craft with a crew of two needs a captain; and since (in beginning canoeing) most of the steering happens in the stern, men jumped into the captain's seat.

Actually, having the brawnier paddler (presumably the man) in the stern is backwards for the way most beginners paddle. Here's why: a canoe doesn't naturally go in a straight line, as you may have noticed in frustration. It naturally veers off toward the side the bow paddler is on, *as if* the stern paddler were working harder. So putting the stronger paddler in the bow is a way of equalizing things. The canoe goes straighter, the stern paddler spends less energy on corrective steering. In other words, brawn in the bow, brains ... no, *finesse* in the stern. Most women can learn the rudiments of steering a canoe in a few hours.

It's not that men should automatically take the bow either. In canoe classes, I often suggest men paddle with other men, and women paddle together; people learn faster when there's a balance in size, strength, and especially style. Many people like to switch positions often, alternating the fun of steering with the joy of spacing out in the bow, pretending you're alone. (Rearrange gear to balance the weight fore and aft in the canoe.) Often both paddlers steer: this is true in white water canoeing, and the bow paddler, who has a clearer view of what's ahead, initiates most moves. Skilled flat-water paddlers often use similar coordinated steering, with the more powerful paddler in the stern, and the bow paddler initiating the turns. It's like dancing together on the water, and, as Mike Galt, designer of elegant canoes, likes to put it, "my lady leads."

If you're a beginner, you don't need to worry about all the different styles. Just remember not to get stuck in the bow, because if you don't start learning how to steer, you might start to think it's because you can't.

People in many other outdoor activities have similar limiting ideas. Back in the '20's, women mountaineers began what was rather quaintly called "manless climbing;" it's not that they wanted to avoid men — it was just their only chance to get to be lead climbers on the rope. In backpacking, being the head map-reader and navigator might be the "power position," one you want to share. Assume that if there seem to be "women's roles," the other ones are more fun; learn to do all parts, to build your confidence.

Carry Your Own Weight

What deters many women from canoeing is the dread of carrying a 75 or 80 pound canoe out of the garage, or between lakes. (Out in the woods, it's called a "portage," but the French doesn't make it easier.) **Two things to keep in mind:** modern materials have made possible lighter weight canoes; and you really can learn to do it. Compensate for brawn with balance, grace and will. Skinny, teen-age girls carry canoes; plump middle-aged women do too. It just takes some imagination, and getting the hang of it.

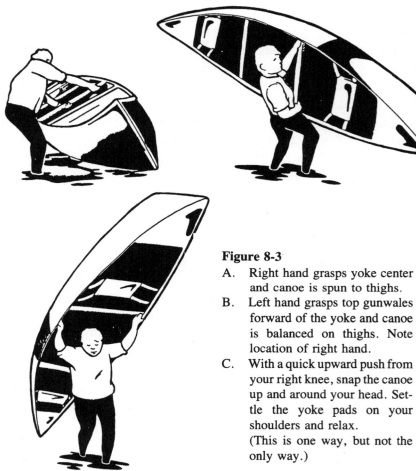

Figure 8-3
A. Right hand grasps yoke center and canoe is spun to thighs.
B. Left hand grasps top gunwales forward of the yoke and canoe is balanced on thighs. Note location of right hand.
C. With a quick upward push from your right knee, snap the canoe up and around your head. Settle the yoke pads on your shoulders and relax.
(This is one way, but not the only way.)

One of my favorite portage memories is of gray-haired Jean, who said, *"This is a ball!"* the first time she carried a canoe alone. Back in Boston, her horrified friends had asked how she was getting ready for the wilds of Minnesota. *"Watching Mary Tyler Moore re-runs,"* she said. She was a total novice, with great spirit. Soon after, we came across a young woman sitting daintily on a rock while husband and sons, just weedy little kids, carried all their gear. Jean, who was 25 or 30 years older, picked up a canoe and almost ran up the trail. ("I thought she needed a role model," she confided later.) The young woman sighed wistfully, *"Now that's something I've never mastered."* Then she added thoughtfully, *"Of course, I've never actually tried."*

If you haven't watched another woman carry a canoe solo, or rappel down a rock face, or sling on a heavy pack, you might not believe you can do it. Actually, *doing* them isn't so hard. Learning how to do it, the smart way, is what matters.

The main problem with a canoe, for example, is just getting it up overhead. Books will tell you to stand with it cradled on your thighs, get the right grip, and with a decisive shove, flip it over your head. Don't! Women can do this, of course, but unless you have good upper-body strength and some athletic confidence, you won't have the conviction to pull off this maneuver. Instead, two or three people can do this together, dropping it on one person's shoulders for carrying.

Or divide up the motions, since lifting and twisting simultaneously is what can send you off to the chiropractor. A group of Iowa women had canoed hundreds of miles together before they ever read about The Correct Way. So they invented the obvious, easy way: turn the canoe upside down, with the stern on grass or shrubs so it won't get scratched; two women stand on opposite sides of the bow and lift that end only; one then supports the end while the other moves into carrying position. This method doesn't look nearly so impressive, but they have too much fun to care.

In any outdoor sports, watch other women to see how they've learned to handle weight. Many women get a backpack on by the inelegant method of sitting on the ground, pack propped against a rock or tree. They shrug into the pack, and get a friend to give them a hand up. I find this tiring, but when there's a friendly rock or log at hand, like to boost a pack on top of it before sliding into the straps.

Equipment and Resources

Don't be put off by gear-snobs: a good canoe is one you can own and use; any canoe on the water is worth two in the store. However, if all you have used is a large, flat-bottomed aluminum canoe, at least try out solo boats or slender, faster tandem boats of more graceful lines. There is no one "all-around" canoe — if you are buying, you have to try out a lot first to see what you like. A good source of information is the annual *Buyer's Guide* published by *Canoe* magazine (P.O. Box 10748, Des Moines, IA 50349).

Long before buying a canoe, get your own light weight paddle, since most rental paddles are real clunkers.

There are many good canoe instruction books (none mentioning women much). I recommend: for beginners in canoeing and camping, *The New Wilderness Canoeing and Camping* by Cliff Jacobson (1986, ICS Books); for canoe technique, beginner to advanced, *The Path of the Paddle* by Bill Mason (1983; reissued in 1989 by NorthWord); since it's hard to learn physical skills from even such a well-illustrated book, the *Path of the Paddle* videotapes on quiet-water and white water (available from NorthWord) are even better. Articles on sophisticated canoe technique that do discuss women paddlers appear in *Canoesport Journal* (P.O. Box 991, Odessa, FL 33556.) Brief historical sketches of women and canoeing, and stories reflecting women's ways of canoeing past and present appear in *Rivers Running Free*, edited by Judith Niemi and Barbara Wieser (1987, Bergamot Books).

APPENDIX I: BOOKS FOR OUTDOOR WOMEN

If you don't know enough outdoorswomen who can teach you, encourage you and inspire you, meet them in books. Besides the books on specific skills mentioned throughout the text, here's some informative and entertaining reading:

GENERAL REFERENCE AND HOW-TO BOOKS (Many of these are out of print, but available in libraries.)

Galland, China. *Women in the Wilderness*. 1980, Harper Colophon Books. A broad survey, with stories from her experience, history, and thoughts on the political and spiritual aspects of women's trips.

LaBastille, Anne. *Women and Wilderness*. 1980, Sierra Club Books, San Francisco. Profiles of several women in outdoor careers.

Link, Sheila. *Women's Guide to Outdoor Sports*. 1982, Winchester Press, Tulsa. Basic how-to in many sports, including fishing, archery, hunting.

Maugham, Jackie Johnson with Kathryn Collins, M.D. *The Outdoor Woman's Guide to Sports, Fitness and Nutrition*. 1983, Stackpole Books, Harrisburg.

Nichols, Maggie. *Wild, Wild Women*. 1978, Berkely Windhover Books, New York. An encouraging book, with stories from old *Field and Stream* magazines and from her own experience; discussion of the masculine mystique of the outdoors.

Rinehart, Mary Roberts. *The Out Trail*. 1923, New York. Out of curiosity, you might want to read the encouragement this novelist had for other women of her generation; mostly on horsepacking.

RECENT WOMEN'S ADVENTURES (Just a few varied books among many recently published.)

Aspen, Jean. *Arctic Daughter*. 1988, Bergamot Books, Minneapolis. A young couple's first year living off the land in Alaska (and almost starving). Jean was following in her mother's footsteps [Connie Helmericks, below].

Blum, Arlene. *Annapurna: A Woman's Place*. 1980, Sierra Club Books. The 1978 women's ascent of Annapurna, a successful and tragic venture. Written by the leader with as much attention to the personalities and feelings as to the action. Good bibliography.

Brook, Elaine and Julie Donnelly. *The Windhorse*. 1986, U.S. edition, 1989, Paragon House, New York. Two women, one blind, trek in winter to 18,000 feet in the Himalayas. A story of determination and friendship.

Cobb, Sue. *The Edge of Everest.* 1989, Stackpole Books, Join Sue Cobb on the edge of life on the edge of Everest, for a true story of adventure, despair and determination.

Davidson, Robyn. *Tracks.* 1980, Pantheon Books, New York. A young Australian woman with little previous outdoor experience crosses the outback of Australia with camels. A frank, funny, and moving book.

Fons, Valerie. *Keep It Moving: Baja by Canoe.* 1986, The Mountaineers, Seattle. On two weeks' notice, she joined adventurer Verlen Kruger on a 2400-mile journey around Baja, California in two solo boats. She tells how it changed her life.

Helmericks, Constance. *Down the Wild River North.* 1968, Abridged version, 1989, Bergamot Books, Minneapolis. An experienced outdoorswoman takes her daughters, 12 and 14, on a two-summer journey down Canadian rivers to the Arctic ocean because she believes children need freedom and to grow up with nature.

Irvine, Lucy. *Castaway.* 1983, Dell Publishing, New York. On a whim, Lucy Irvine joins a writer for a year of playing Robinson Crusoe on a South Sea island; she thrived on the harsh experience.

Murphy, Dervla. *Eight Feet in the Andes.* 1983, U.S. edition 1986, Overlook Press, Woodstock, New York. The eight feet belong to irrepressible Irish traveller D. M., her 9-year-old daughter, and the loyal mule, Juana. A 1300-mile journey.

Niemi, Judith and Barbara Wieser, editors. *Rivers Running Free: Stories of Adventurous Women.* 1987, Bergamot Books, Minneapolis. Thirty-six canoe women, from 1900 to the present, write about freedom, companionship, learning, and wilderness. Includes both rugged adventures and first experiences in a canoe.

Sutherland, Audrey. *Paddling My Own Canoe.* 1978, University of Hawaii Press. Solo journeys on the wild northeast coast of Moloka'i. She goes light and simple (a tiny inflatable boat) and reflects on being an adventurous single parent.

OUTDOORSWOMEN OF THE PAST (A few of my favorites among our many adventurous foremothers.)

Arnold, Mary Ellicott and Mabel Reed. *In the Land of the Grasshopper Song: Two Women in Klamath Indian Country in 1908- 1909.* 1957; reissued Nebraska University Press, 1980. It was called the roughest place in the country; they loved it, and the diary of their two year stay is written with freshness and wit.

Bird, Isabella. *A Lady's Life in the Rocky Mountains.* 1879; reissued, with introduction by Daniel Boorstin, 1960, U. of Oklahoma Press. An invalid when at home in Scotland, she thrived on solo travel on horseback in the Rockies — "no region for tourists and women."

Hubbard, Mina Benson. *A Woman's Way through Unknown Labrador.* 1908, NY; reprinted 1981, Breakwater Books, Portugal Cove, Newfoundland. After her husband died attempting this journey, Mrs. Hubbard put together her own expedition with four Indian guides, and wrote with great appreciation of them and the land.
   The story of Laddie and Mina Hubbard and the guide George Elson is wonderfully retold by James West Davidson and John Rugge in *Great Heart*, 1988, Viking, NY.

Jackson, Monica and Elizabeth Stark. *Tents in the Clouds: The First Women's Himalayan Expedition.* 1956, London. An impressive adventure of three Scottish women and a few Sherpas. Delightfully told with British humor and understatement.

Stewart, Elinore Pruitt. *Letters of a Woman Homesteader*, 1913; republished 1961, U. of Nebraska Press. A widow with a small child plans a series of outdoor adventures — the first is having her own homestead in Wyoming.

Underhill, Miriam. *Give Me the Hills.* 1956; paperback edition, 1973, Ballantine, NY. Memories of a long life in the mountains of Europe and North America, as a pioneer of "manless climbing" and with her husband.

Vyvyan, Lady C.C. *Arctic Adventure.* 1961, London. Two Englishwomen without canoe experience paddle tributaries of the Yukon in 1926; she writes ecstatically and with humor about the land and the experience.

APPENDIX 2: MAIL ORDER SOURCES FOR BOOKS, INFORMATION NETWORKS

Backcountry Bookstore Box 191, Snohomish, WA 96290. A very extensive catalog of books, maps and videos from many publishers.

Outdoor Woman Patricia Hubbard, P.O. Box 834, Nyack, NY 10960. A newsletter for women of all ages, skill levels, issued 10 times a year, beginning in 1990. $30.

Women in the Wilderness Judith Niemi, 566 Ottawa Avenue, St. Paul, MN 55107 (612) 227-2284. Sells selected books by women adventurers and on outdoor skills. Bibliographies of women wilderness travellers, past and present.

Women Outdoors 55 Talbot Avenue, Medford, MA 02155. National network with local chapters. $15/year, quarterly newsletter. Has a list of women's outdoor programs around the country, reading lists.

Women's Sports Foundation Information and referral service 1-800-227-3988. May be able to help you locate sports and outdoors organizations near you.

WorkAbles for Women Deborah Evans Crawford, Oak Valley, Clinton, PA 15026-0214. (412) 899-3555. Boots, gloves, socks, pants — in women's sizes.

INDEX